3300

PARIAH

November 2022, I was assigned to the Rylands Building on Market Street, Manchester. What was once Debenhams department store, now closed.

Working under Arthur, our task was to disconnect the electricity supply and make the premises safe for the demolition team — the interior of building was being dropped, from the top down. Wandering around in the pitch black with torches, we explored each floor to locate the distribution boards. Stock was strewn around, mannequins askew, definitely creepy. Arthur was ex-army, but in his words: "I used to be a leader of men, now I'm running around in Debenhams shitting myself."

On the third floor, I discovered an office — three desks down the side wall and at the far end a smaller room with a toughened glass screen, behind which they must have kept cash. Upon entering I saw a scattered mass of documents and personal possessions on the carpet. Amongst the detritus numerous photographs. Closer inspection revealed a series of 35mm images — here presented in the following pages. Documentation of an aftermath.

Arthur said: "You'd better keep them."

Nirvana Heire, June 2023

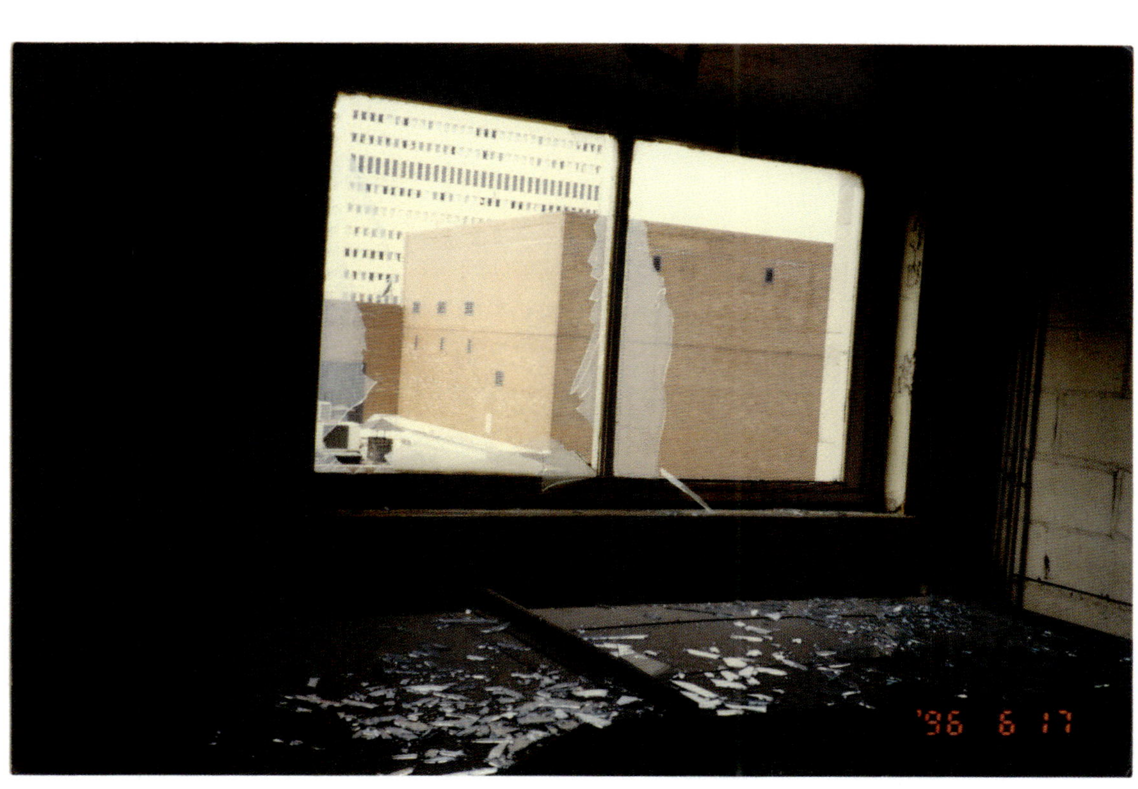

I

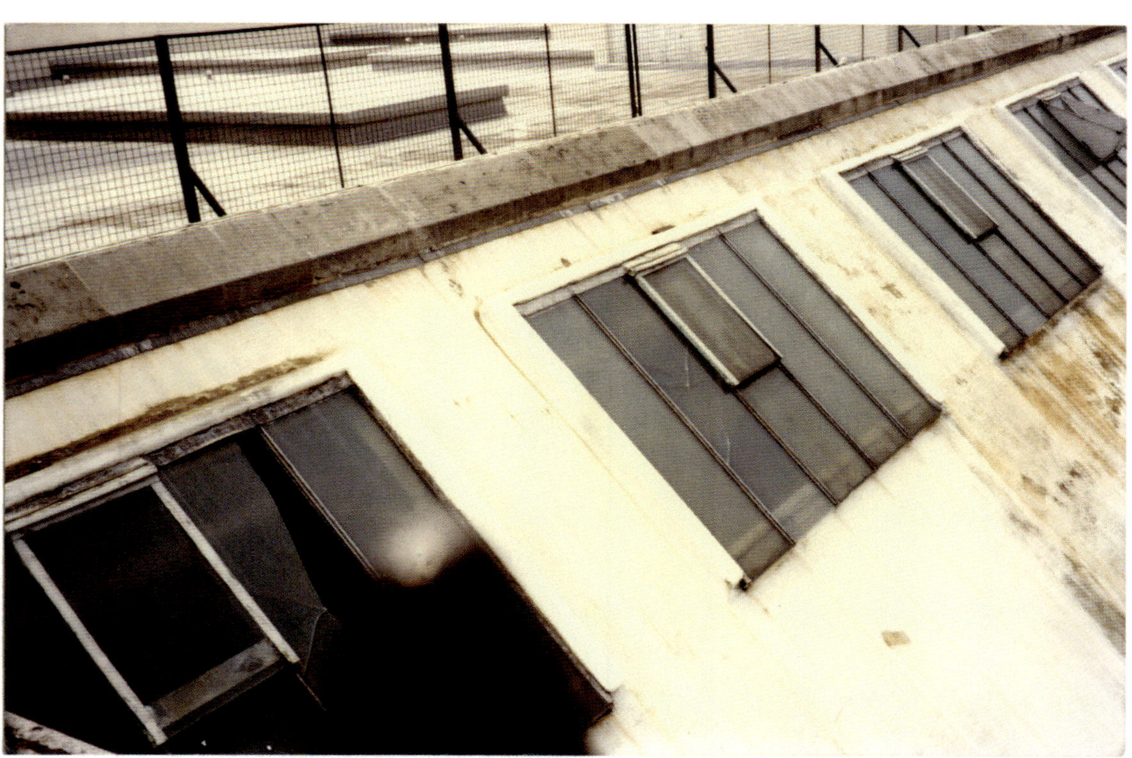

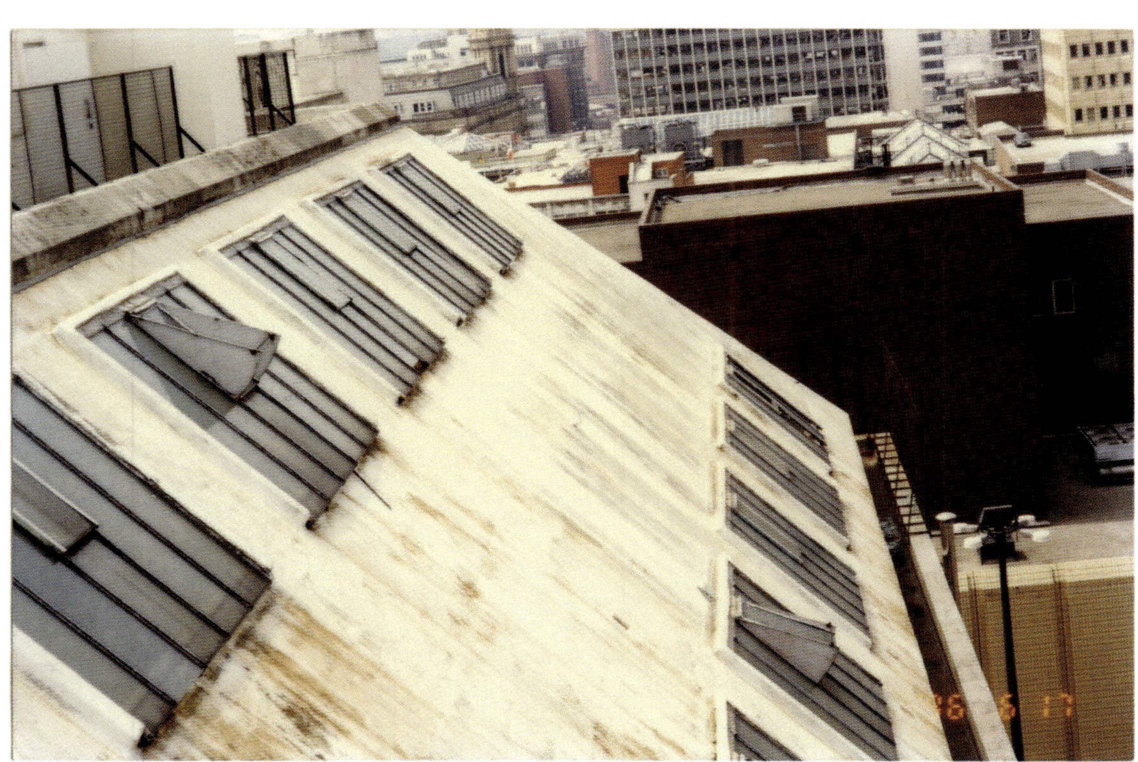

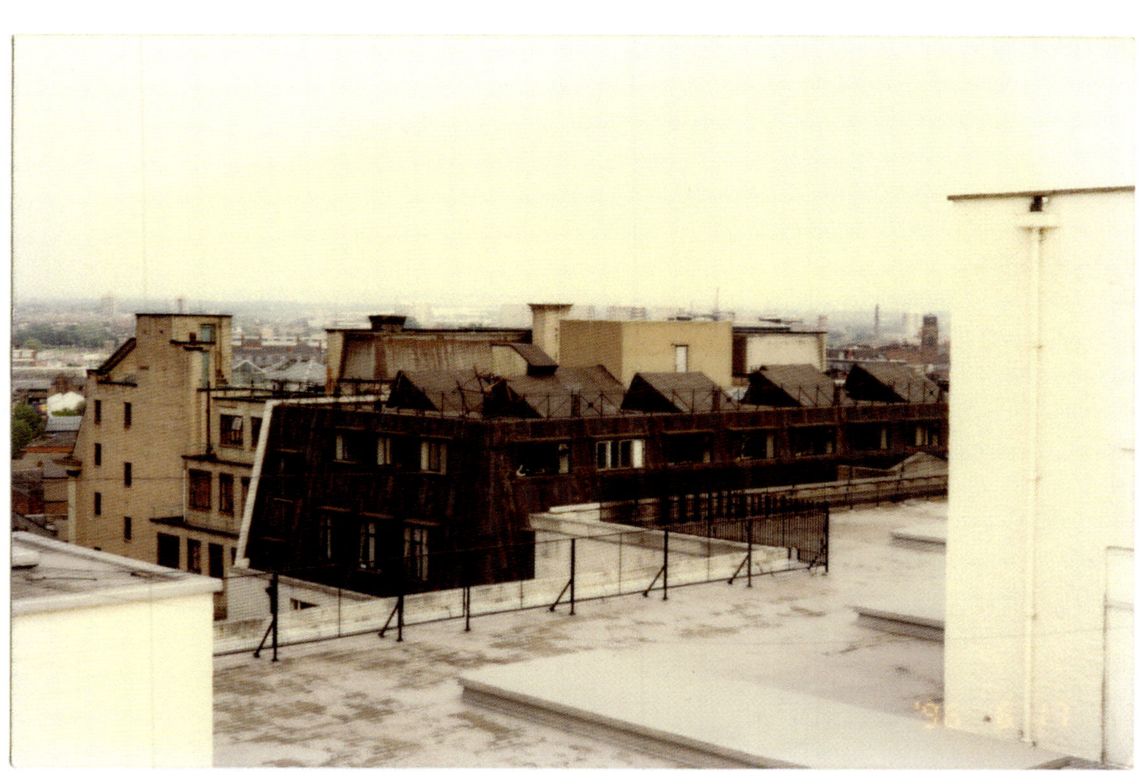

IV

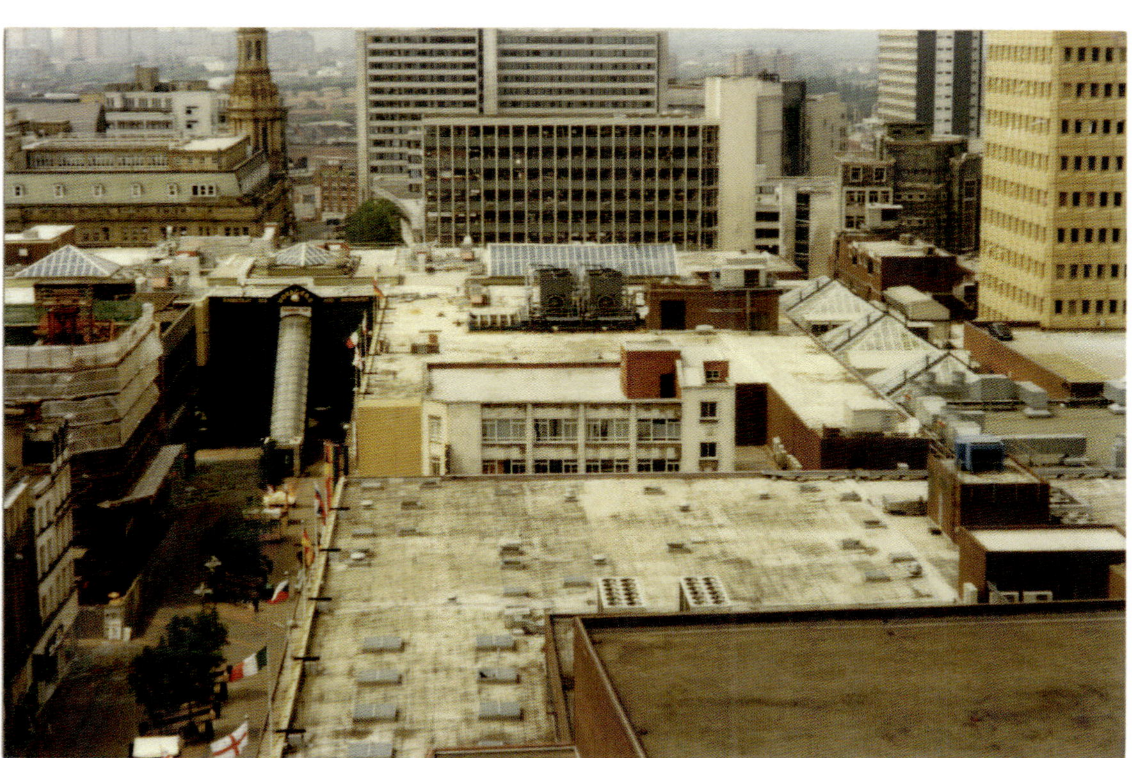

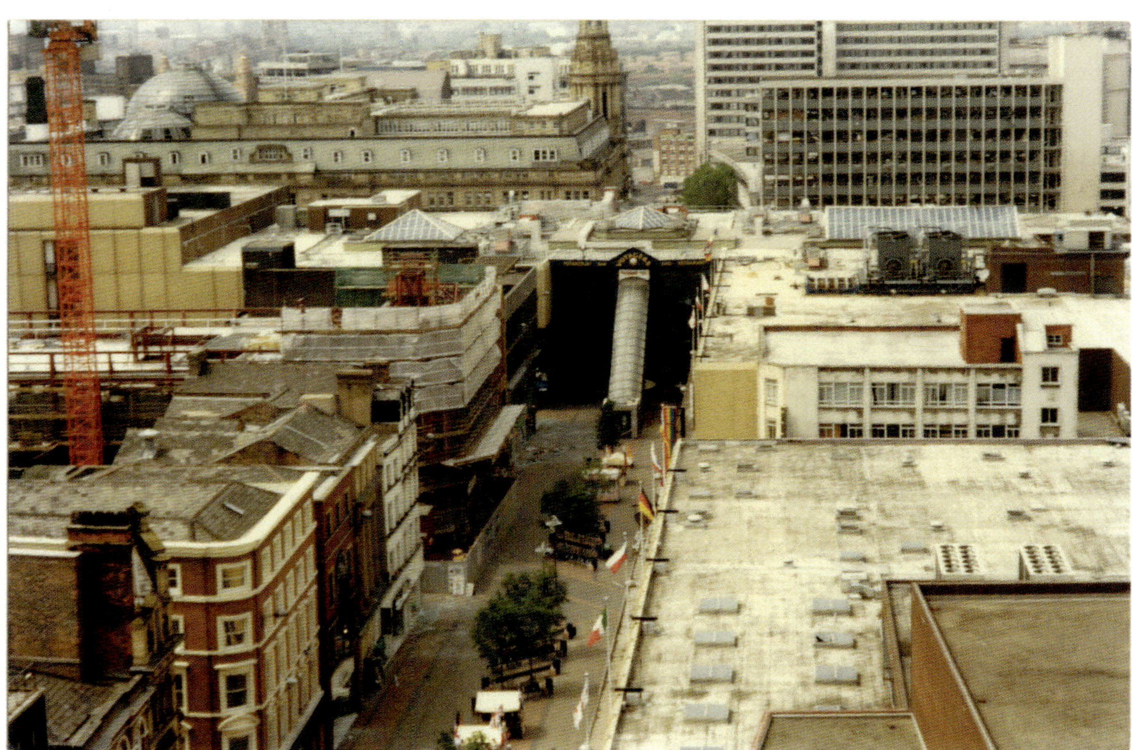

VI

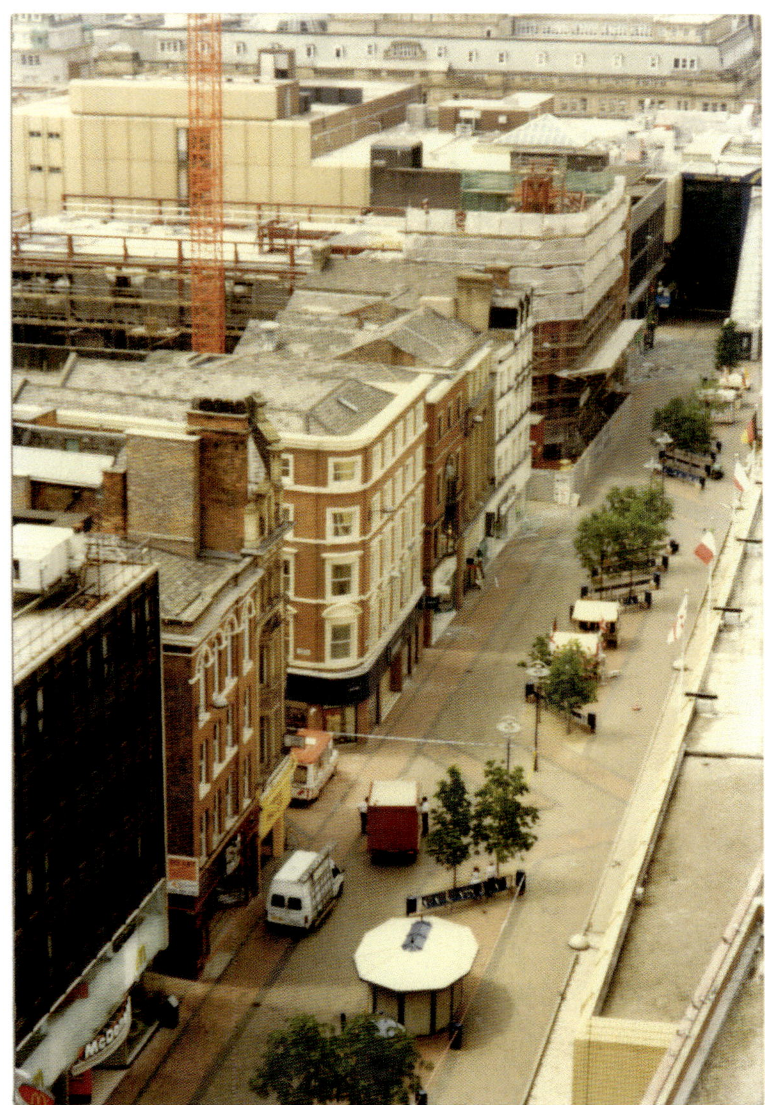

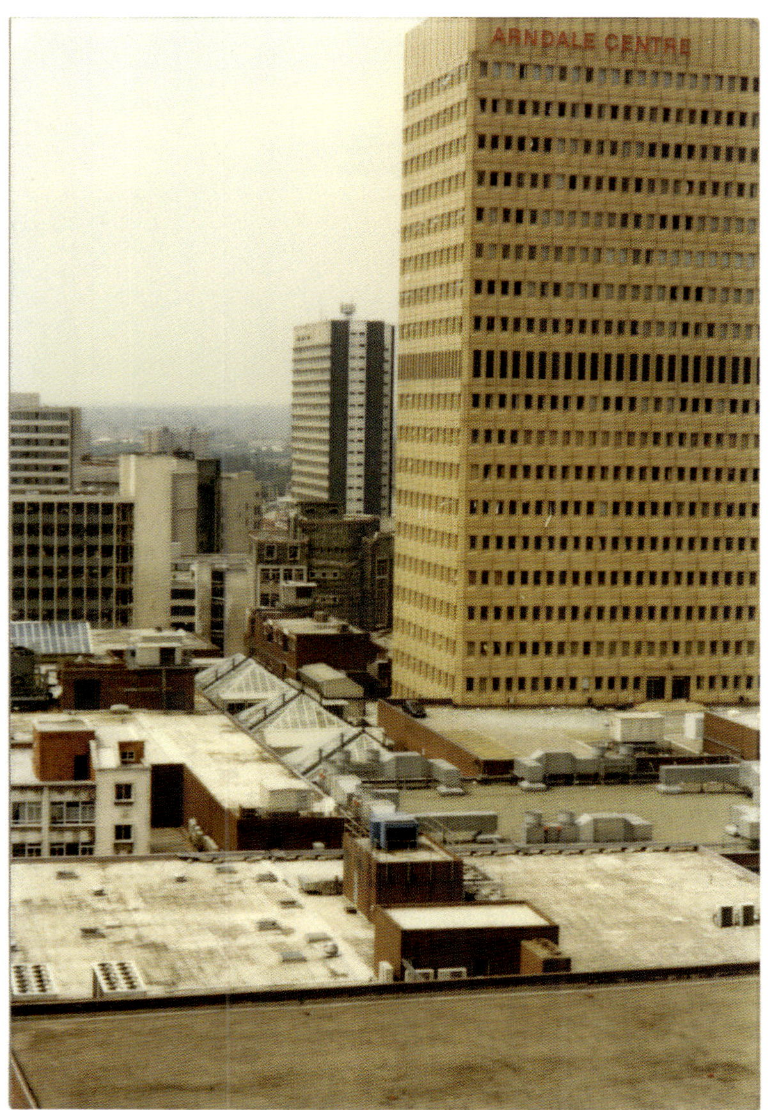
ARNDALE CENTRE

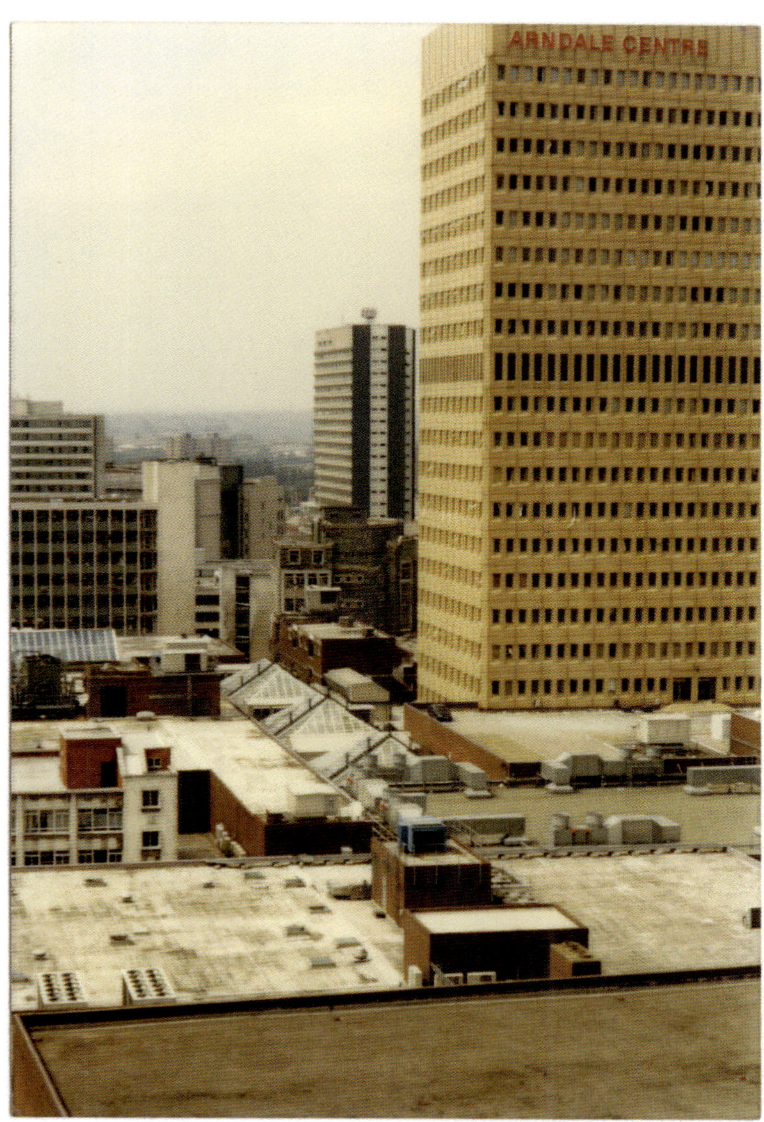
ARNDALE CENTRE

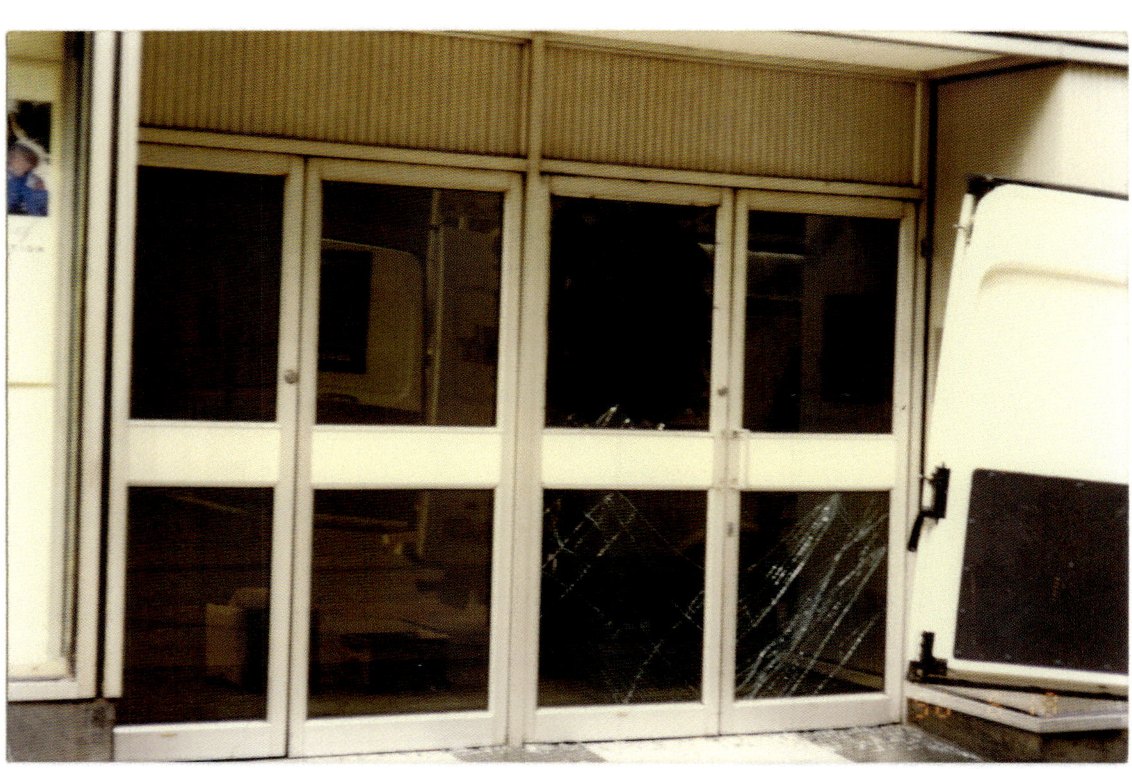

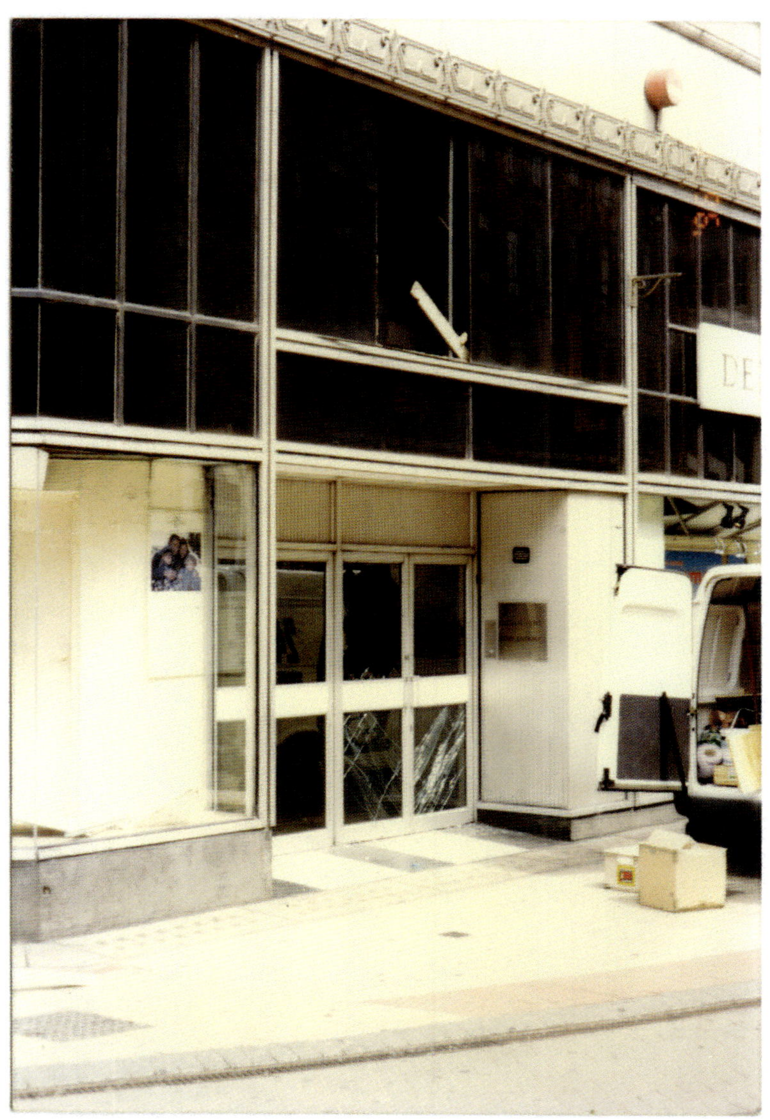

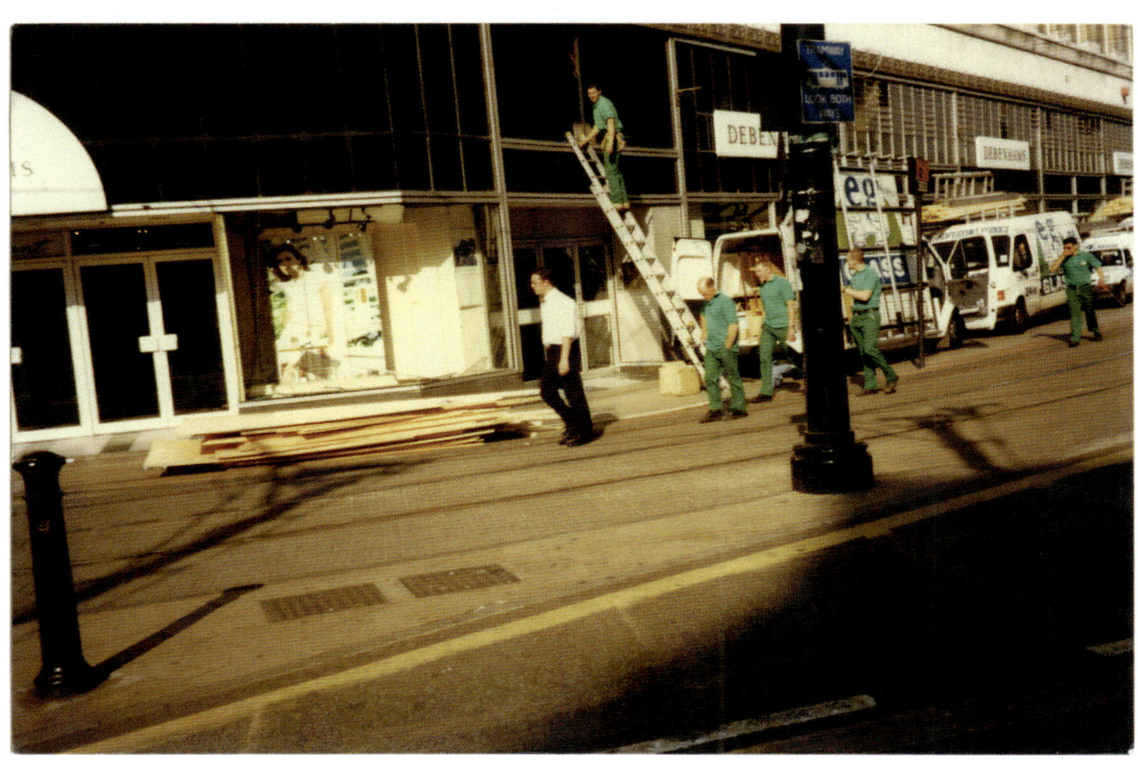
DEBEN

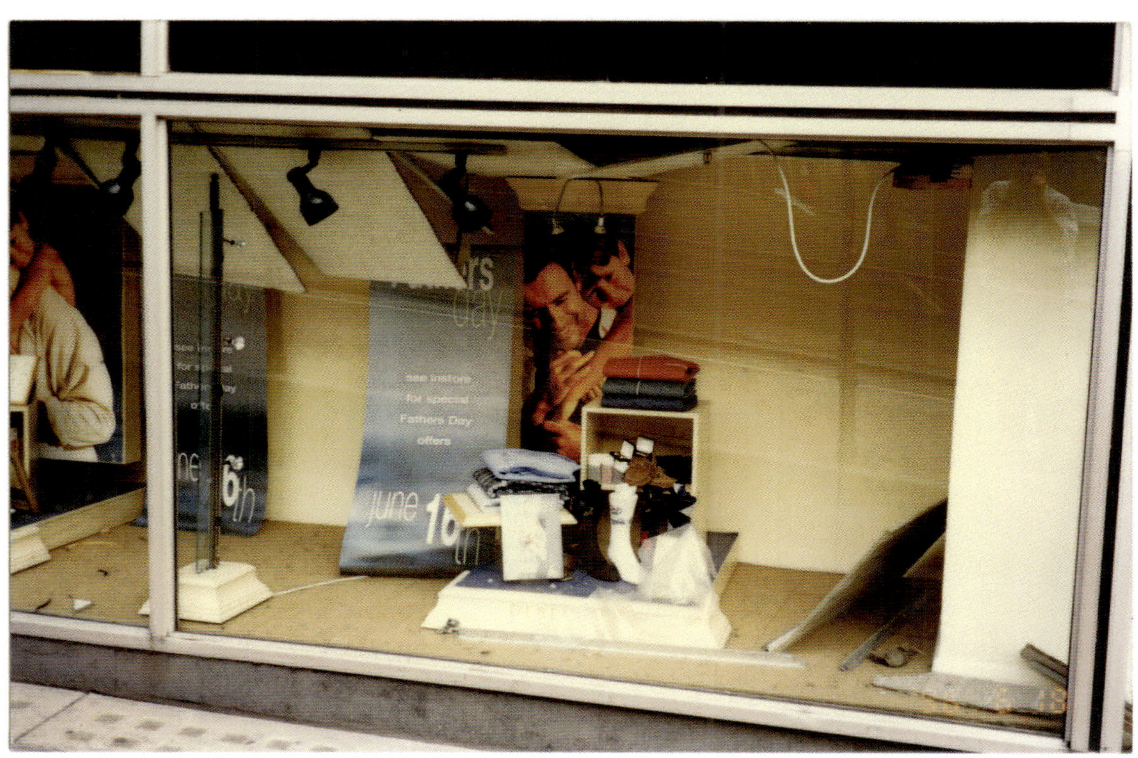
day
see instore
for special
Fathers Day
offers
june 16th

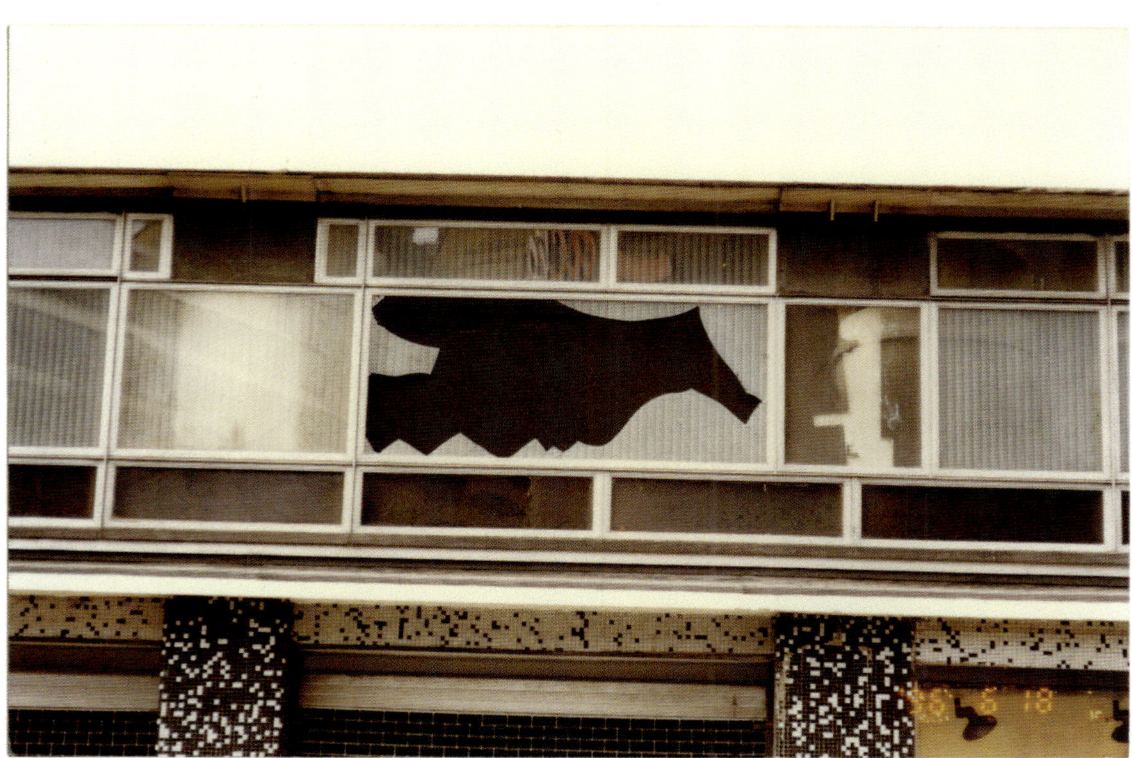

XIV

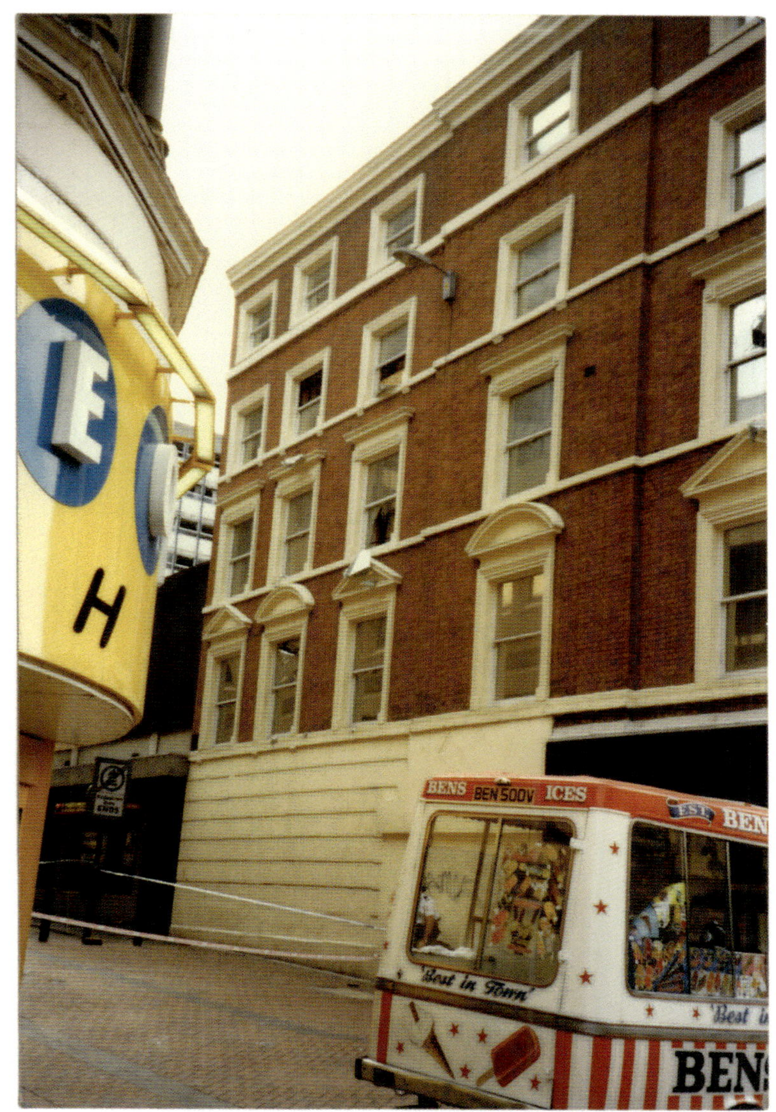
E
H
BENS
BEN500V
ICES
'Best in Town'

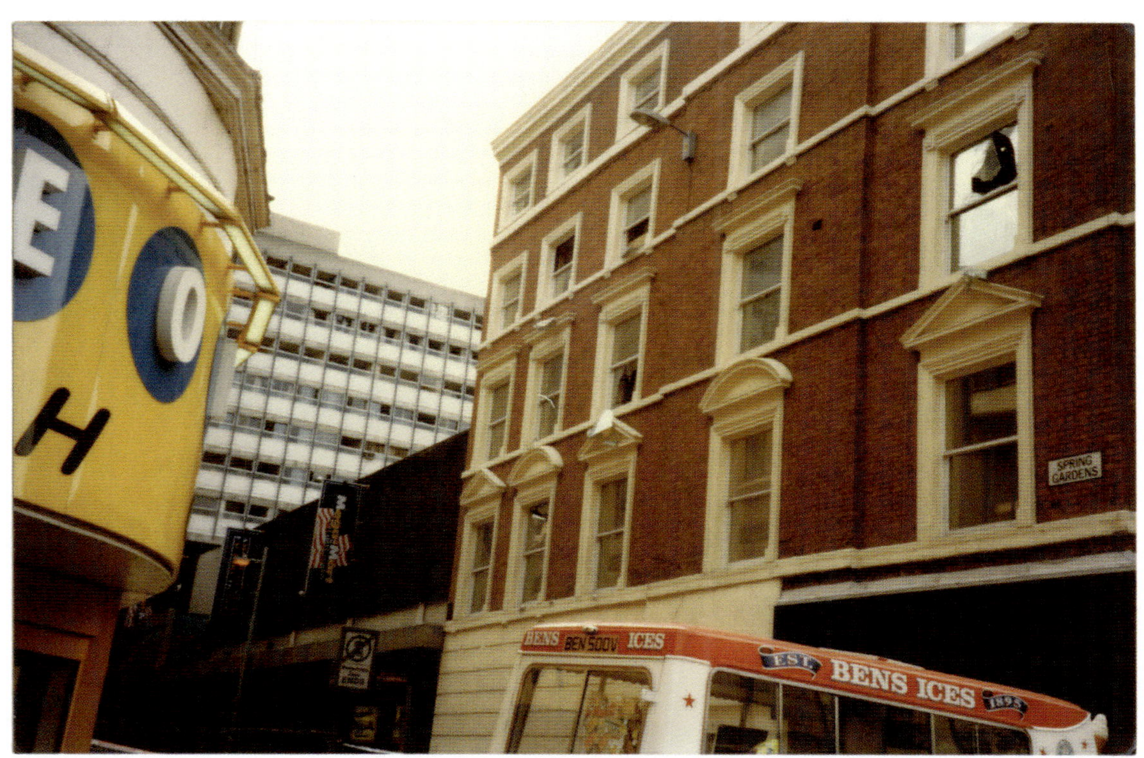

XVI

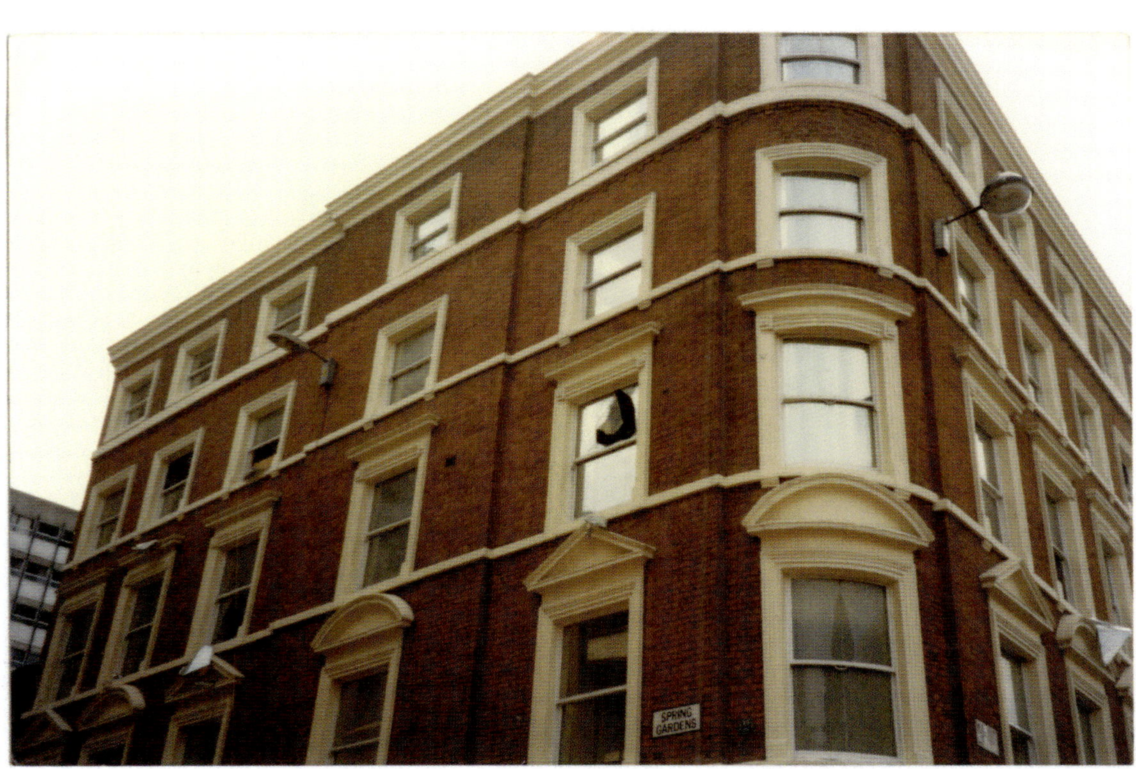
SPRING
GARDENS

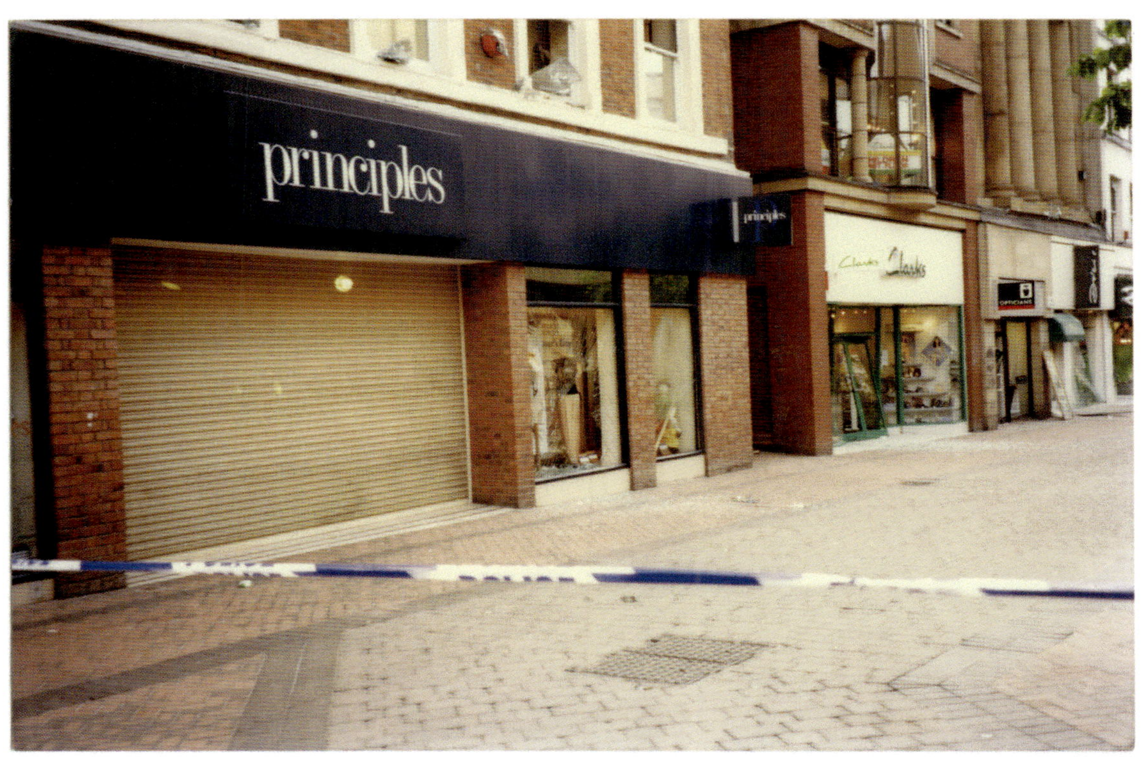
principles
principles
Clarks
OPTICIANS

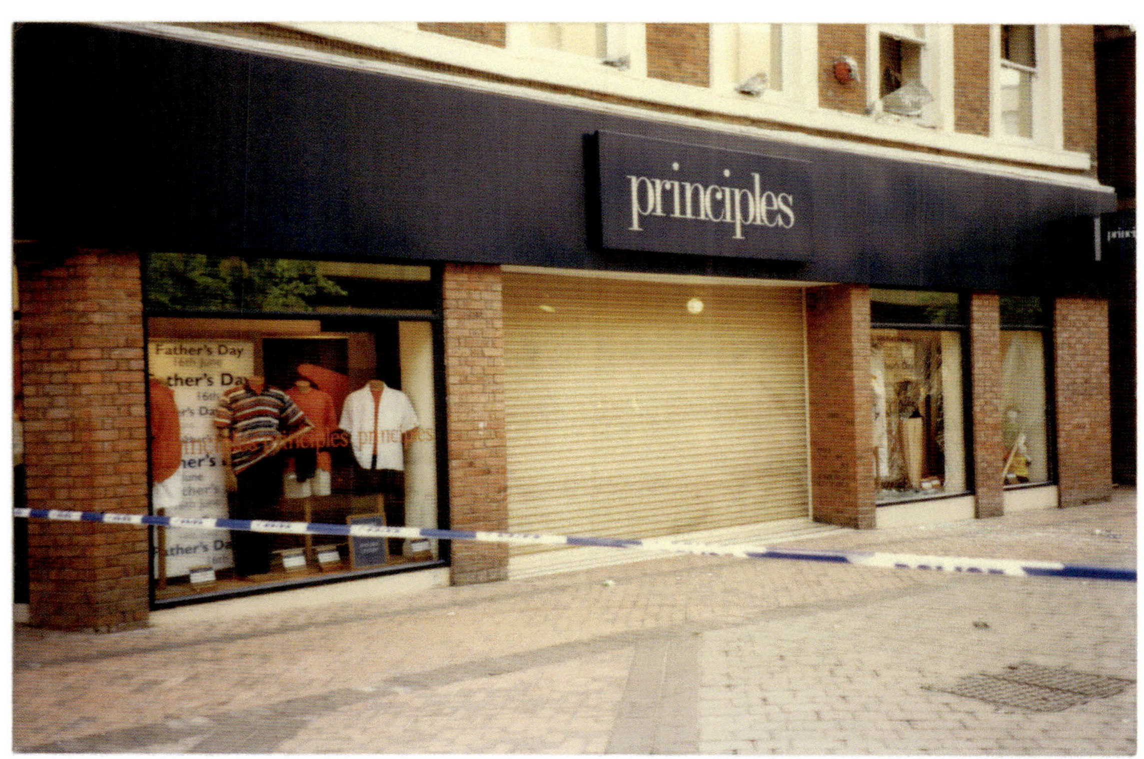
principles
Father's Day

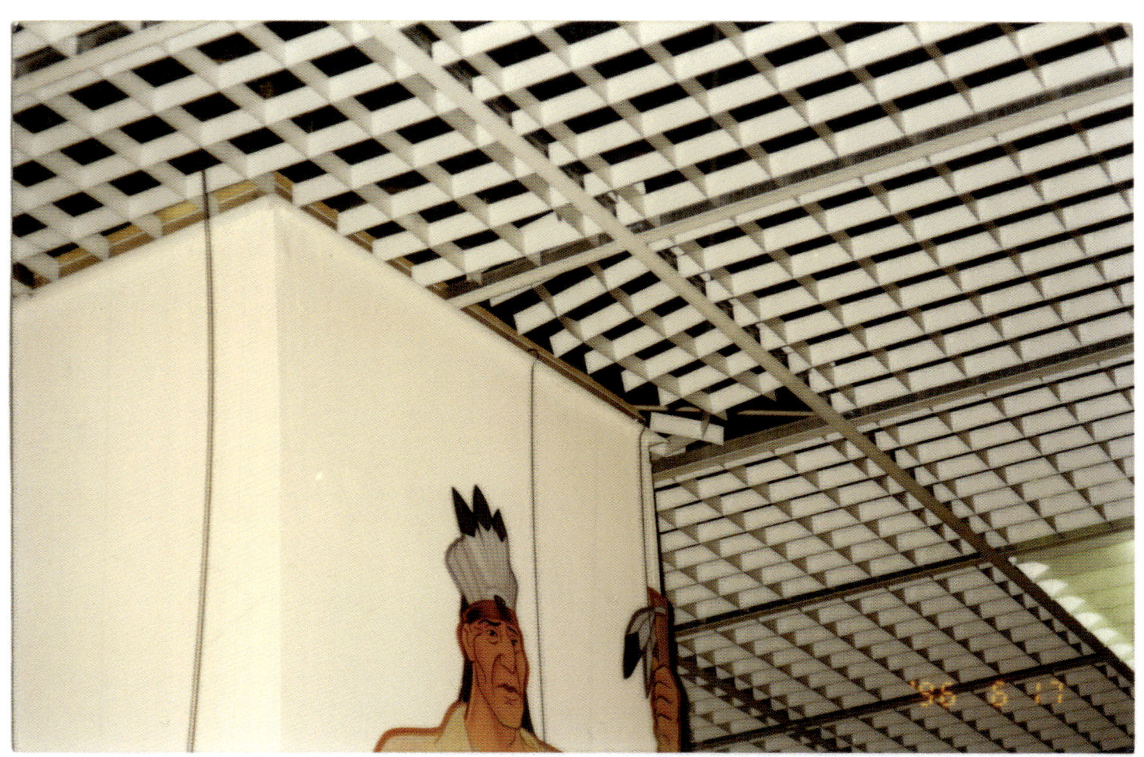
'96 6 17

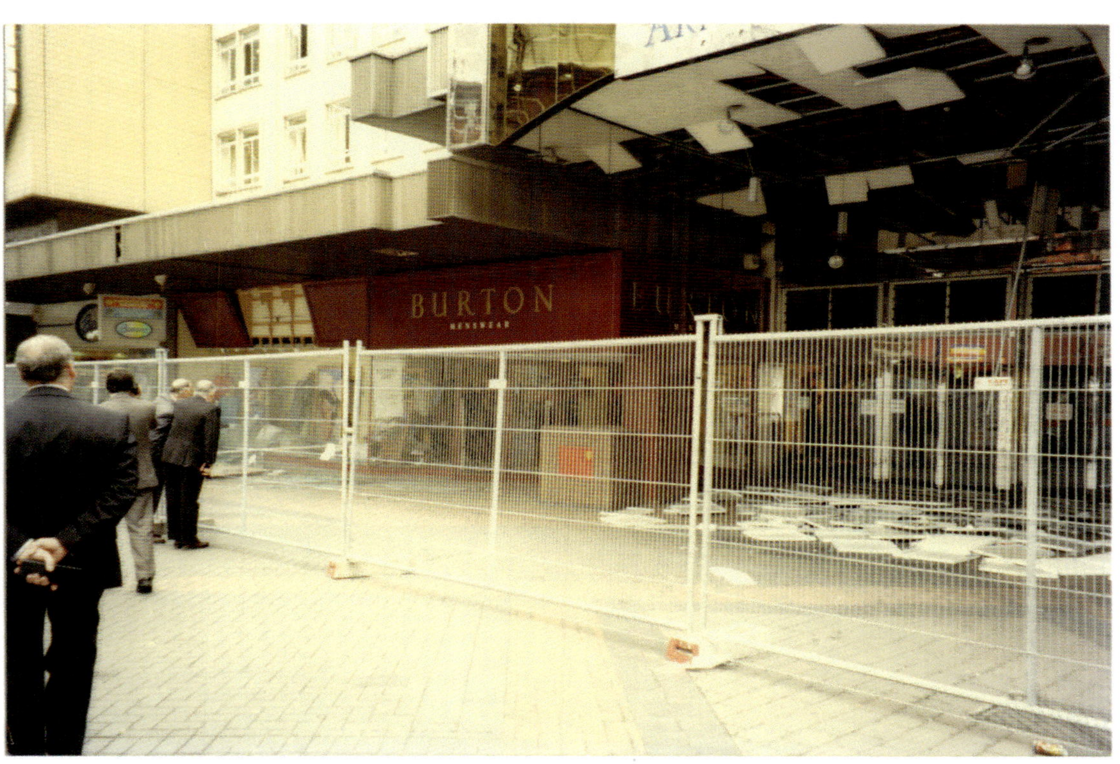

XXI

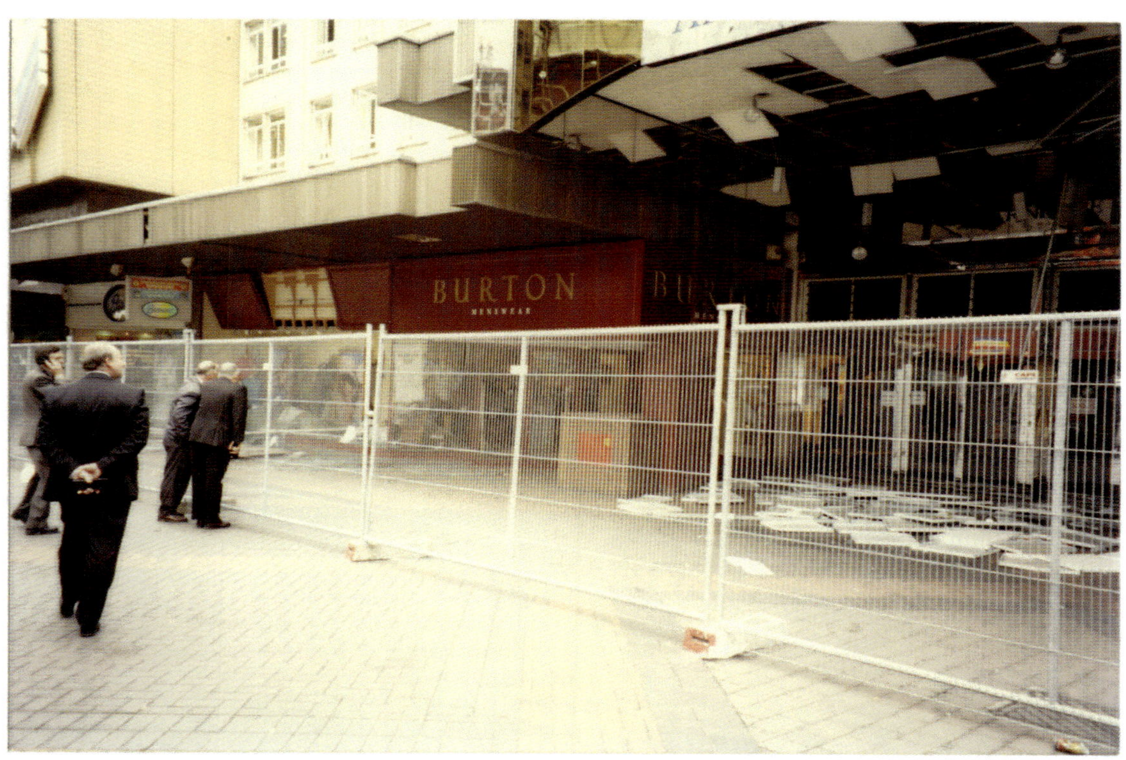
BURTON

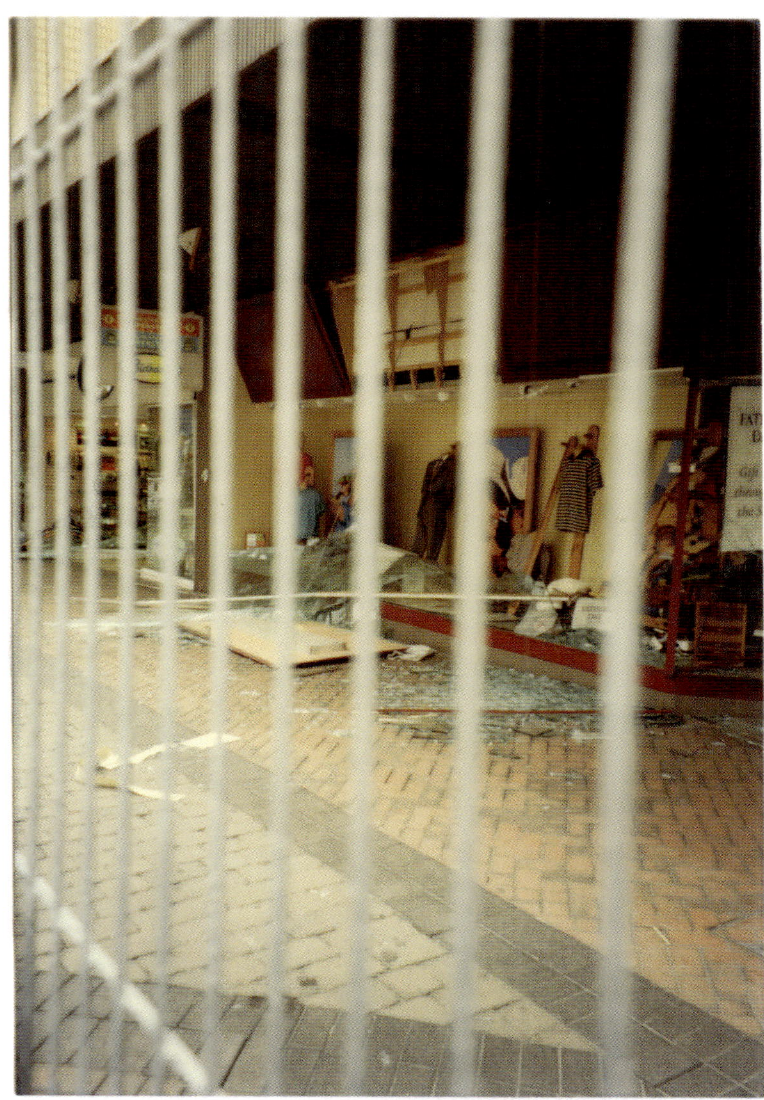

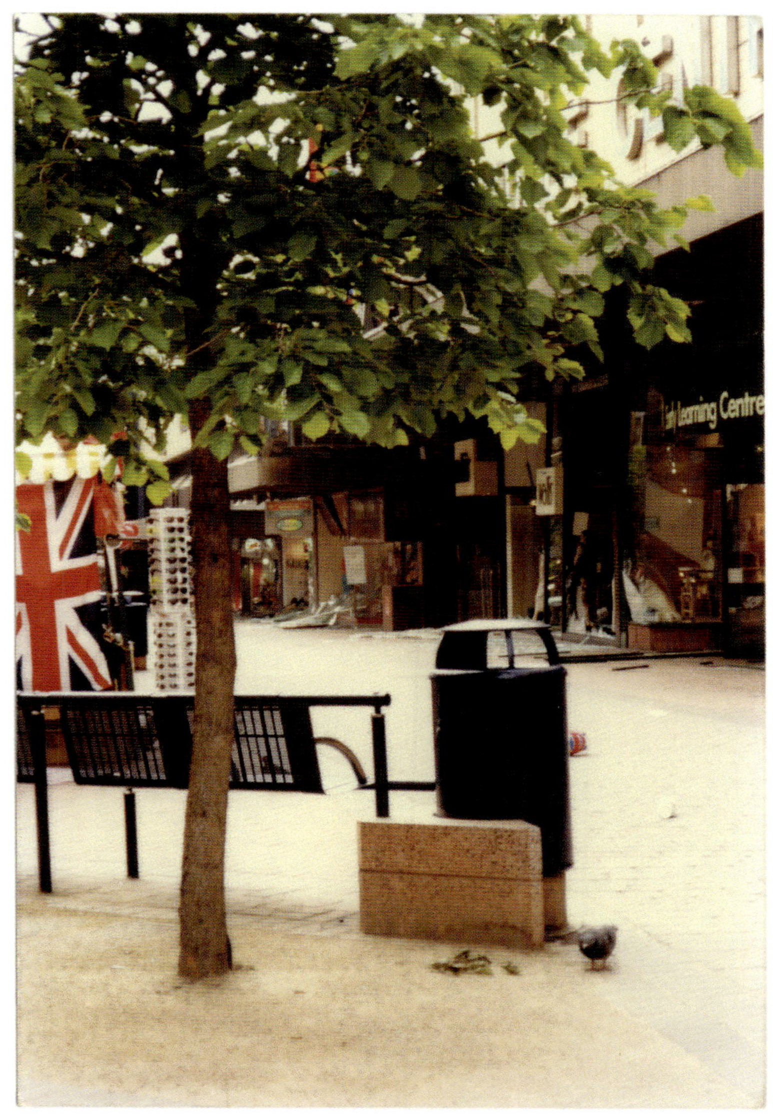
Learning Centre

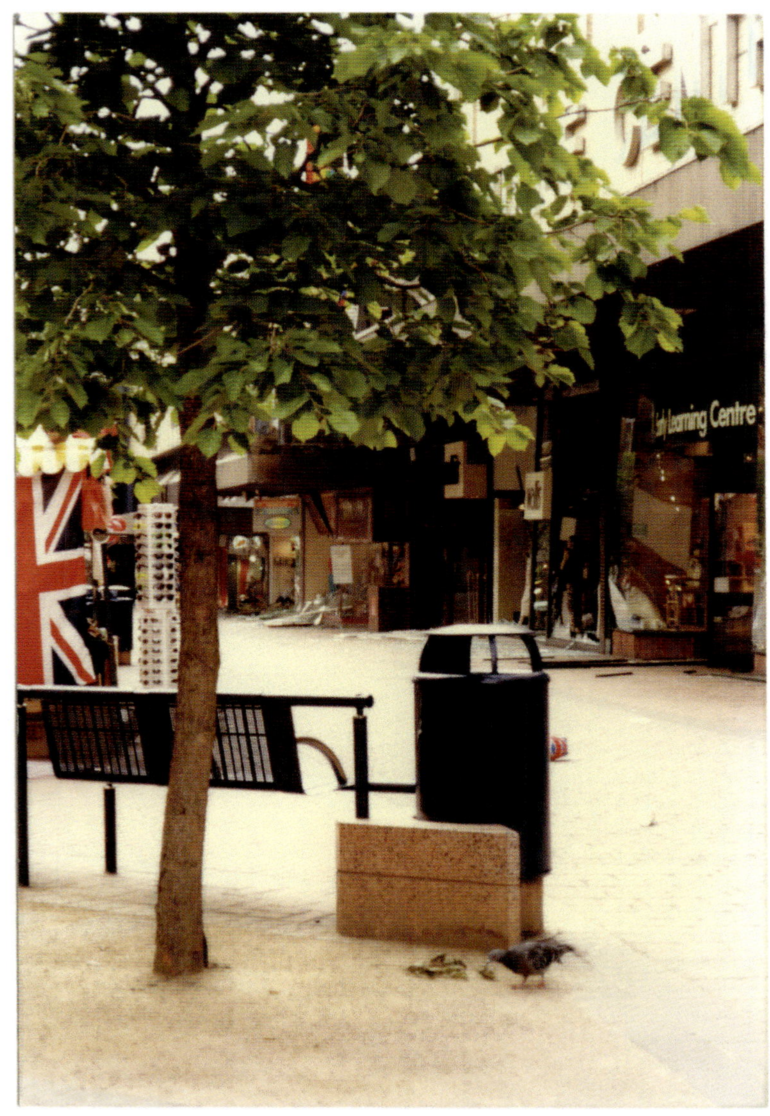
Centre

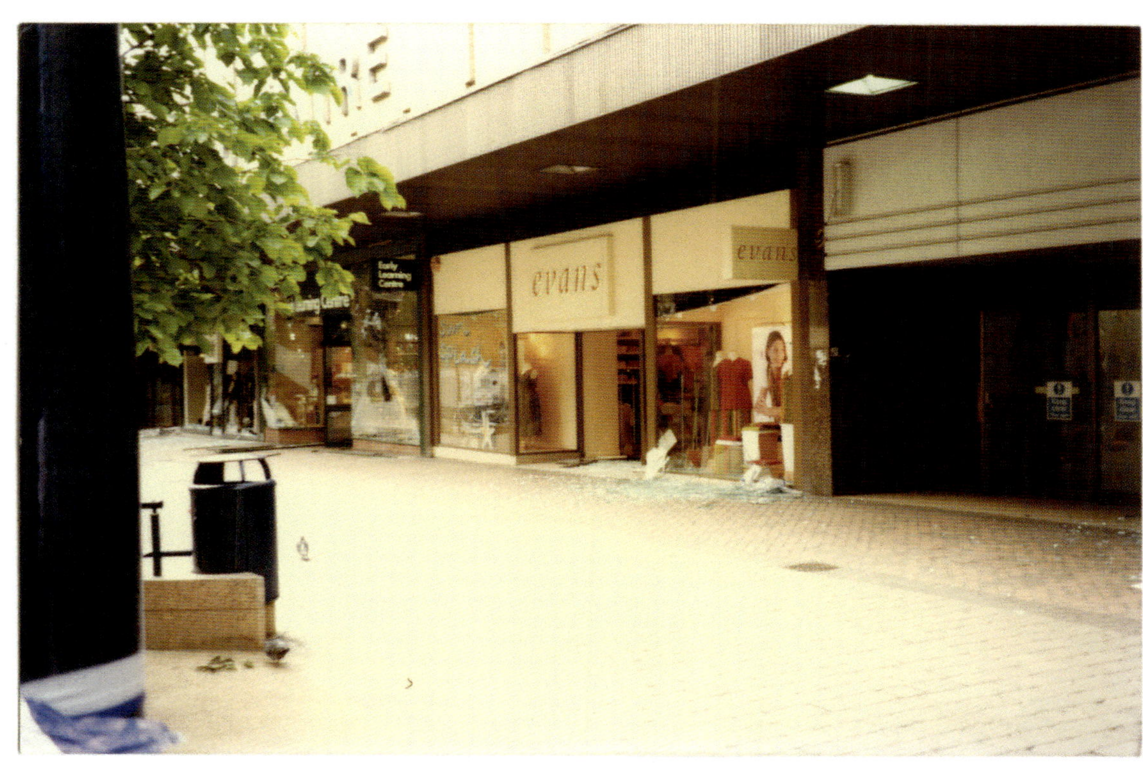

XXVI

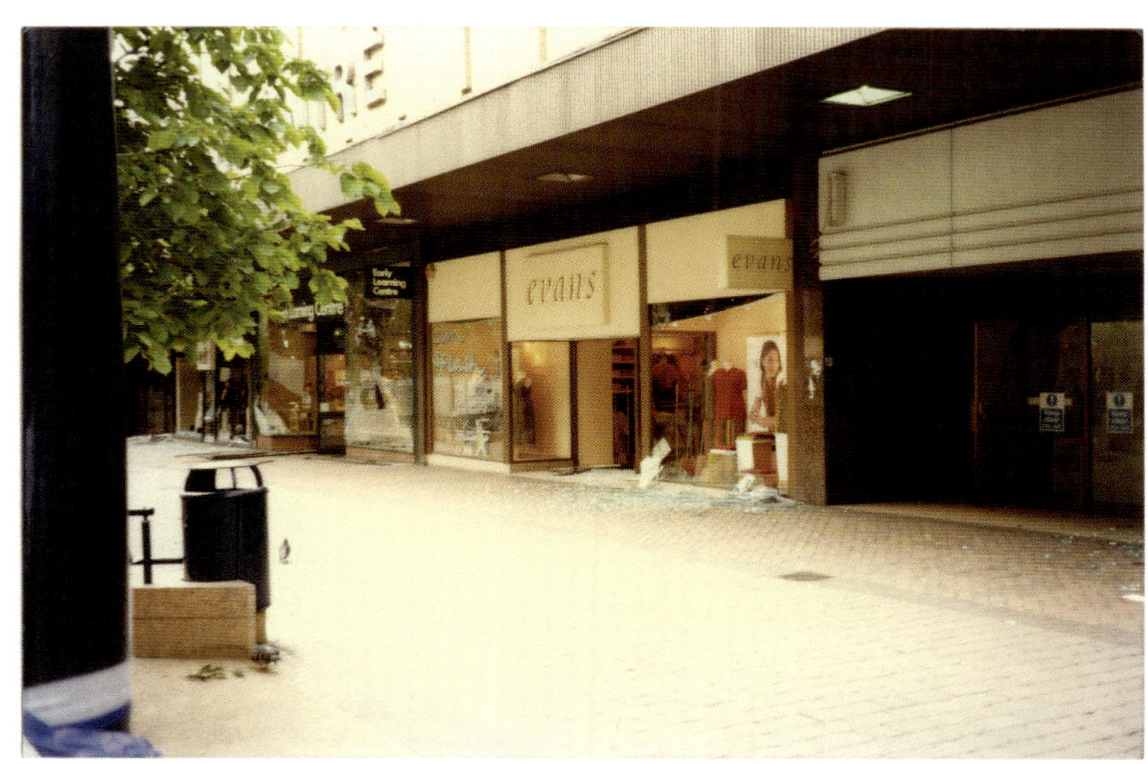

XXVII

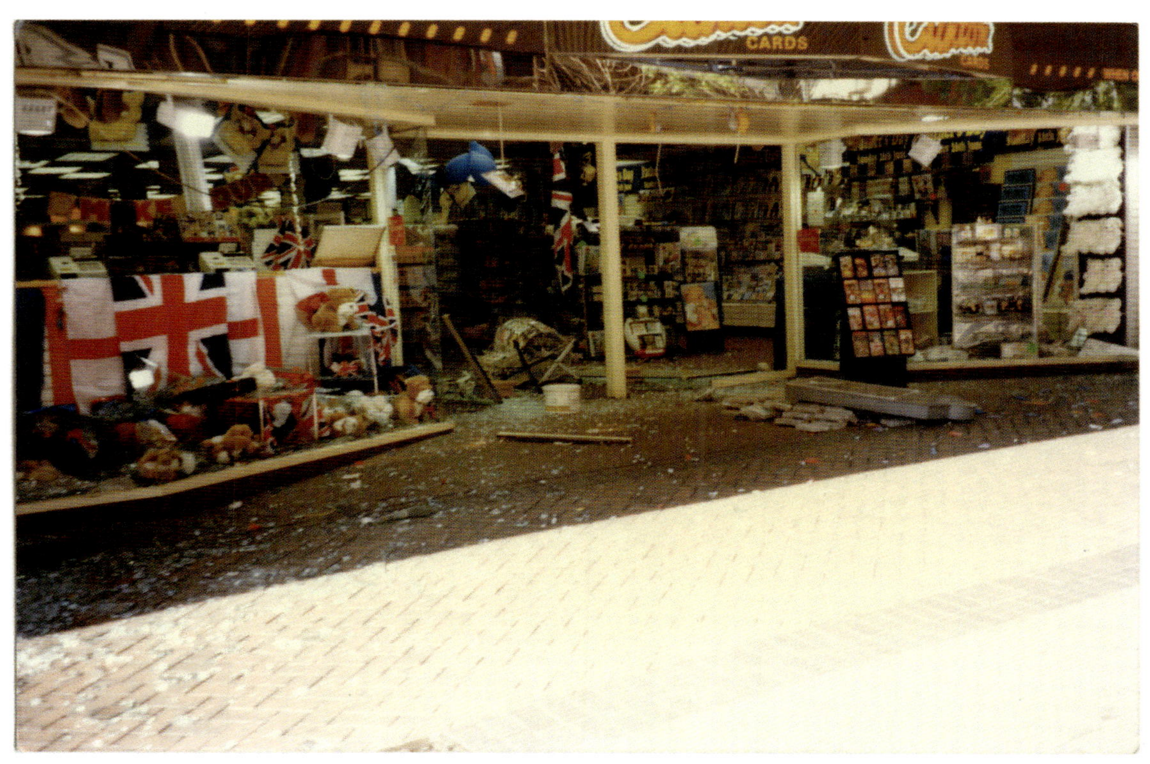
CARDS

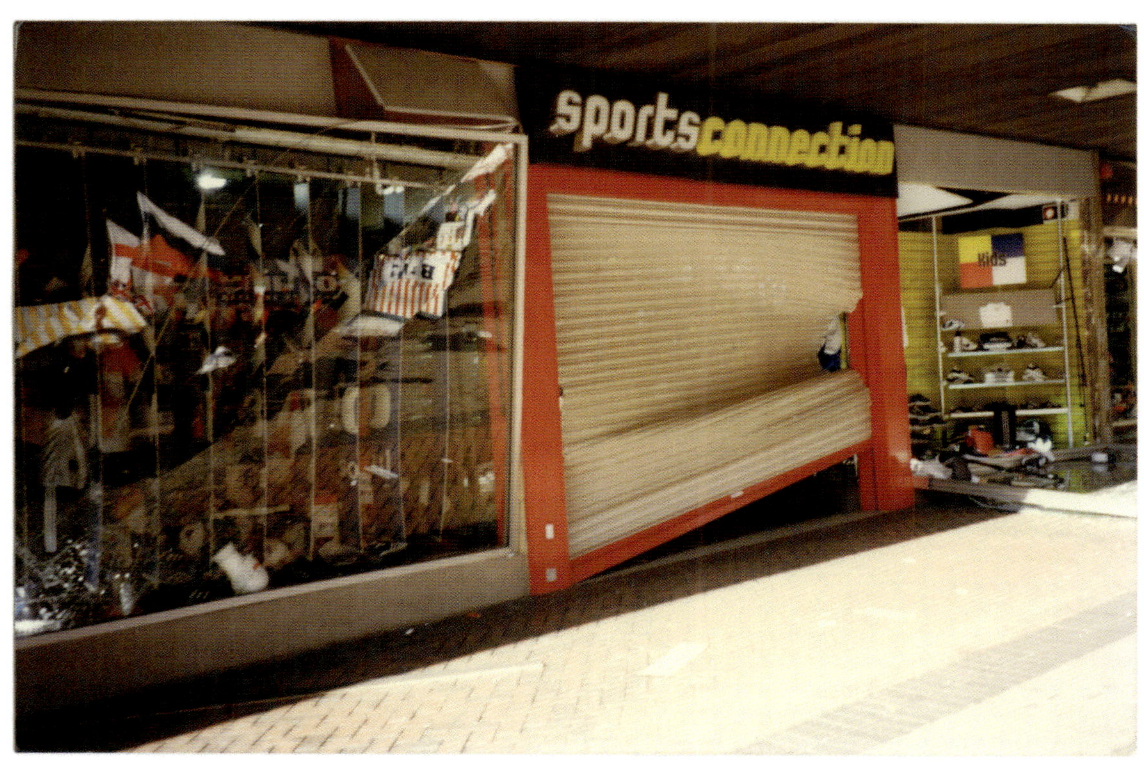
sportsconnection
Kids

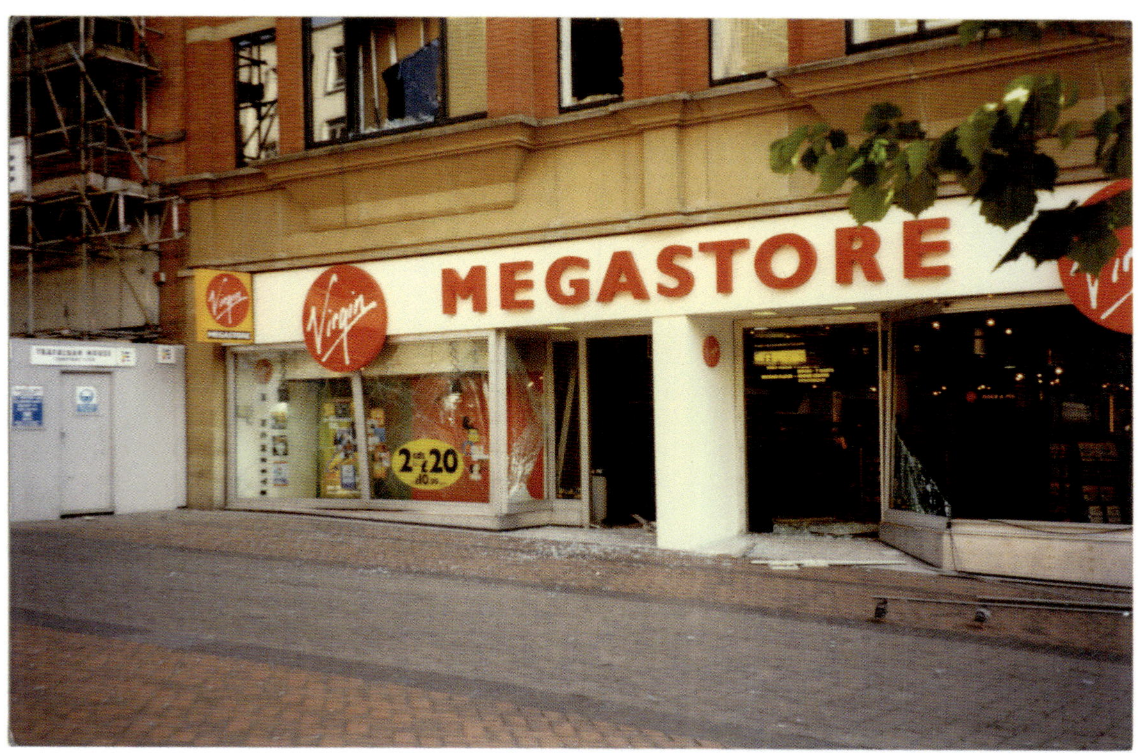

xxx

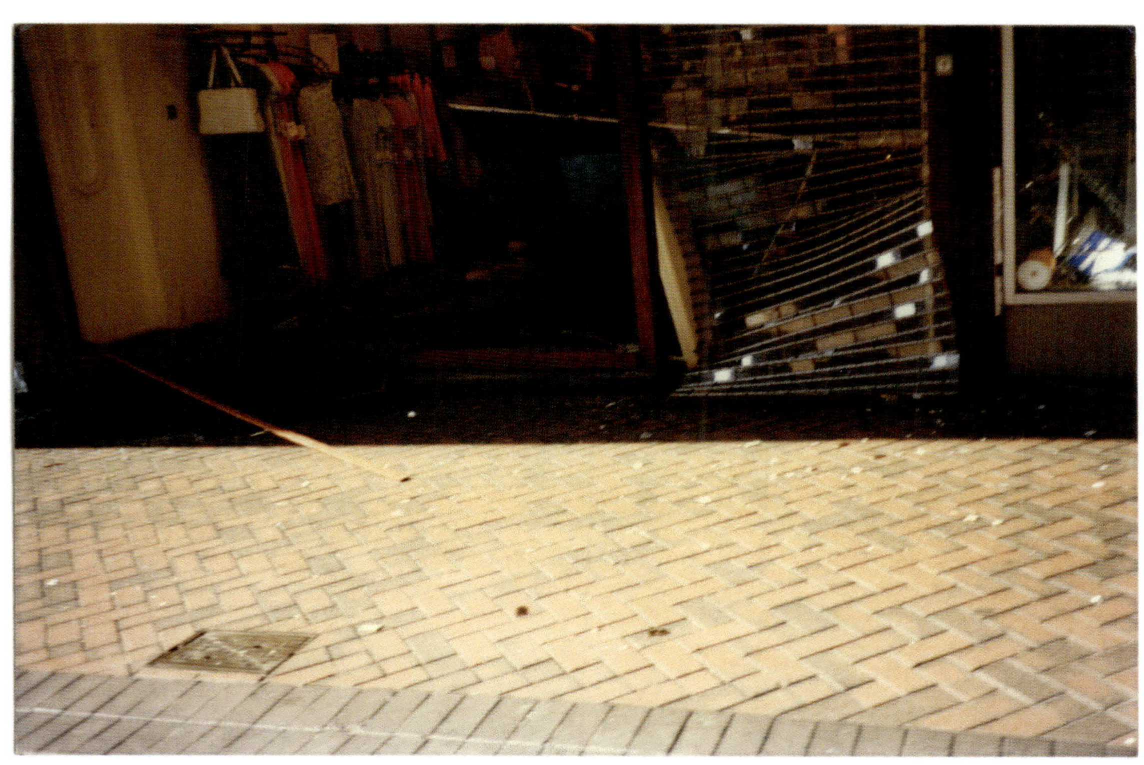

XXXI

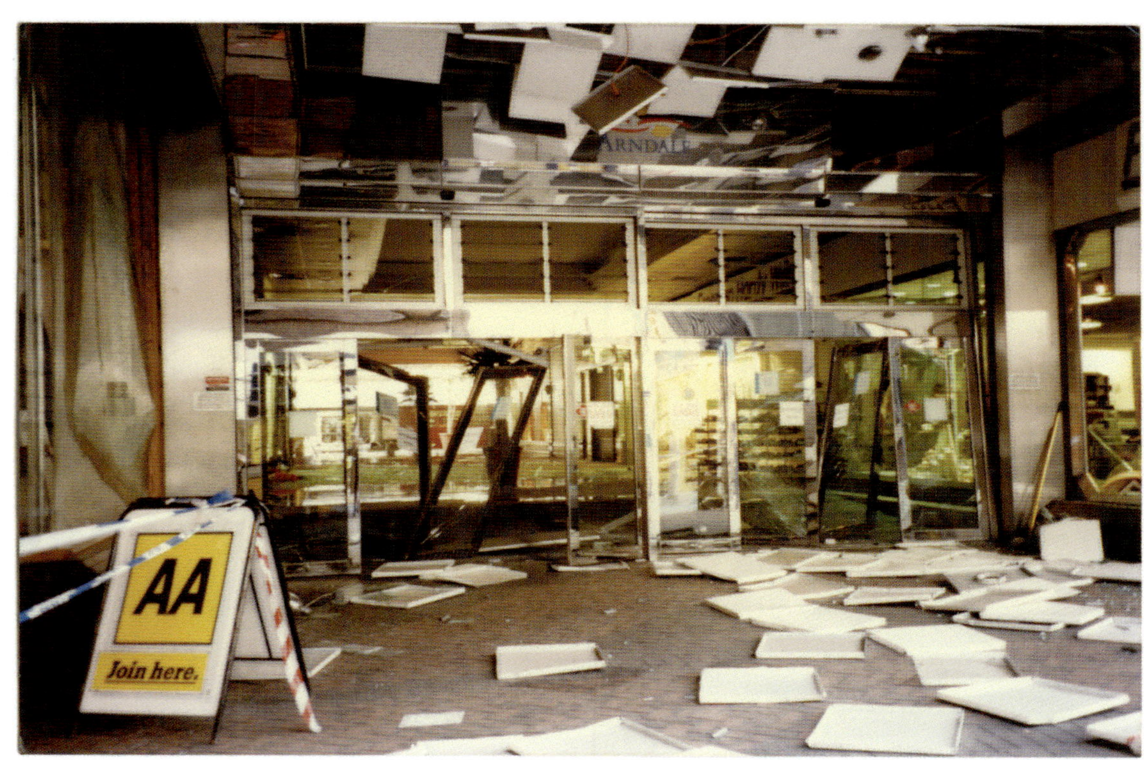
ARNDALE
AA
Join here.

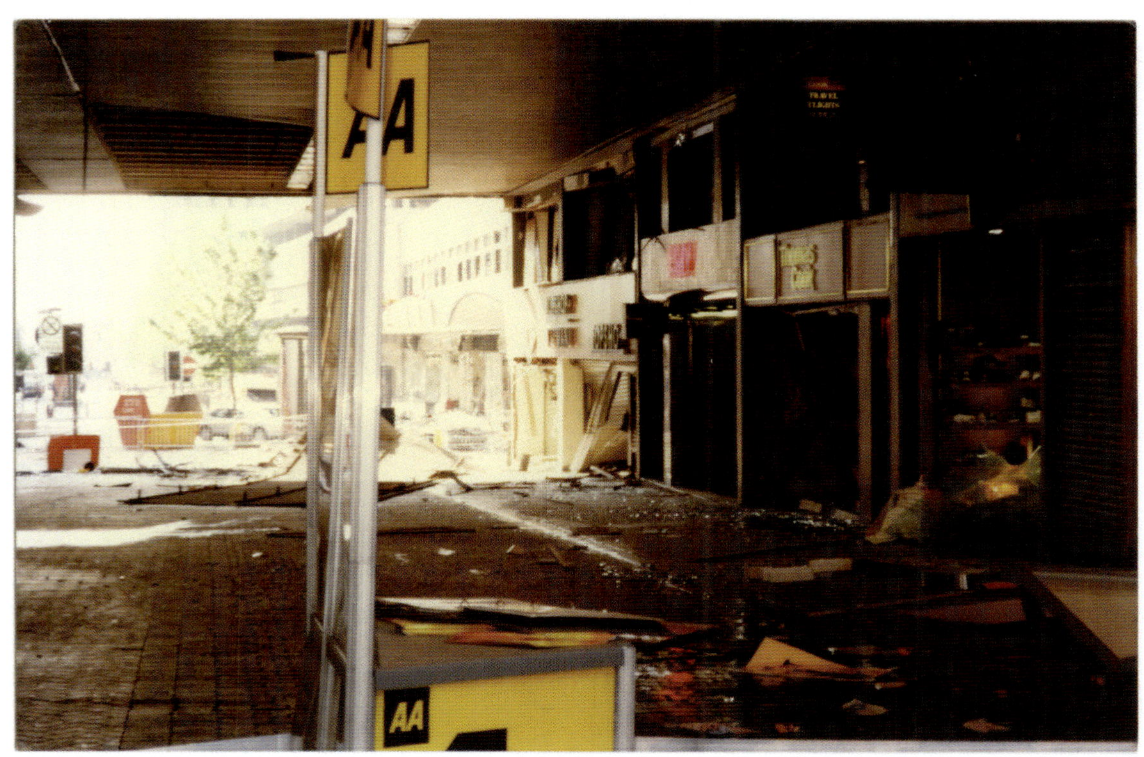
AA
AA

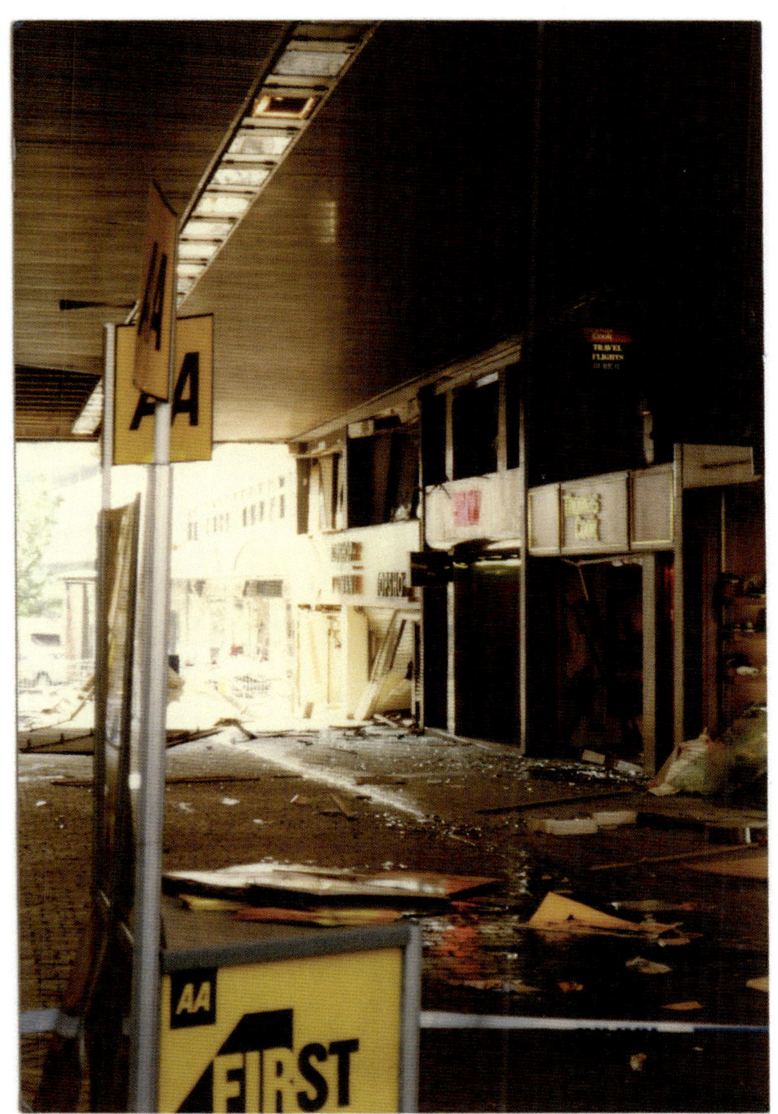
AA
AA
AA
FIRST

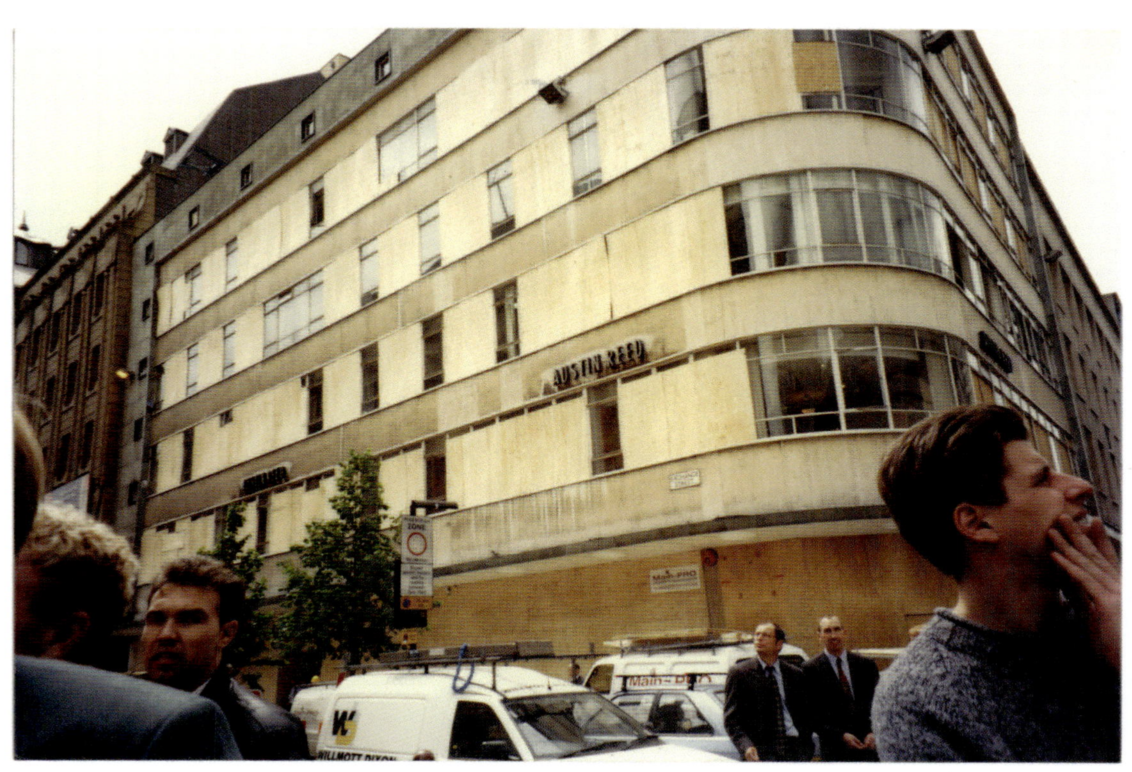
AUSTIN REED
ZONE
WILLMOTT DIXON

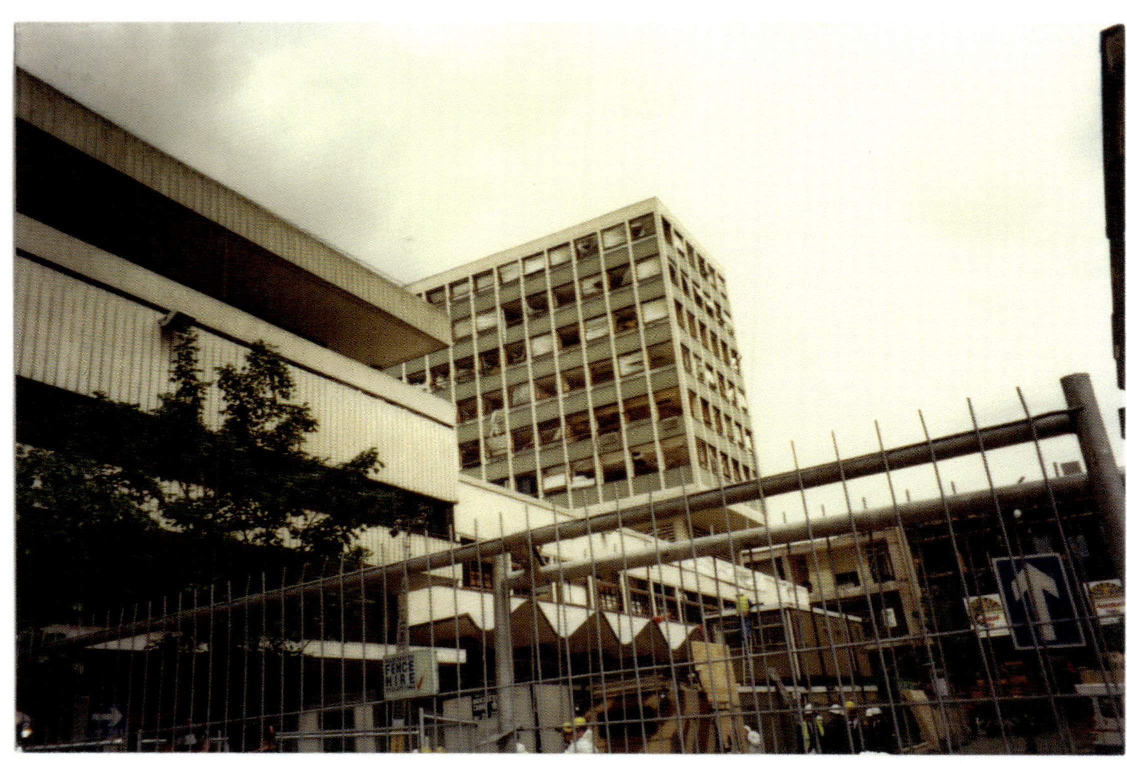
FENCE
HIRE

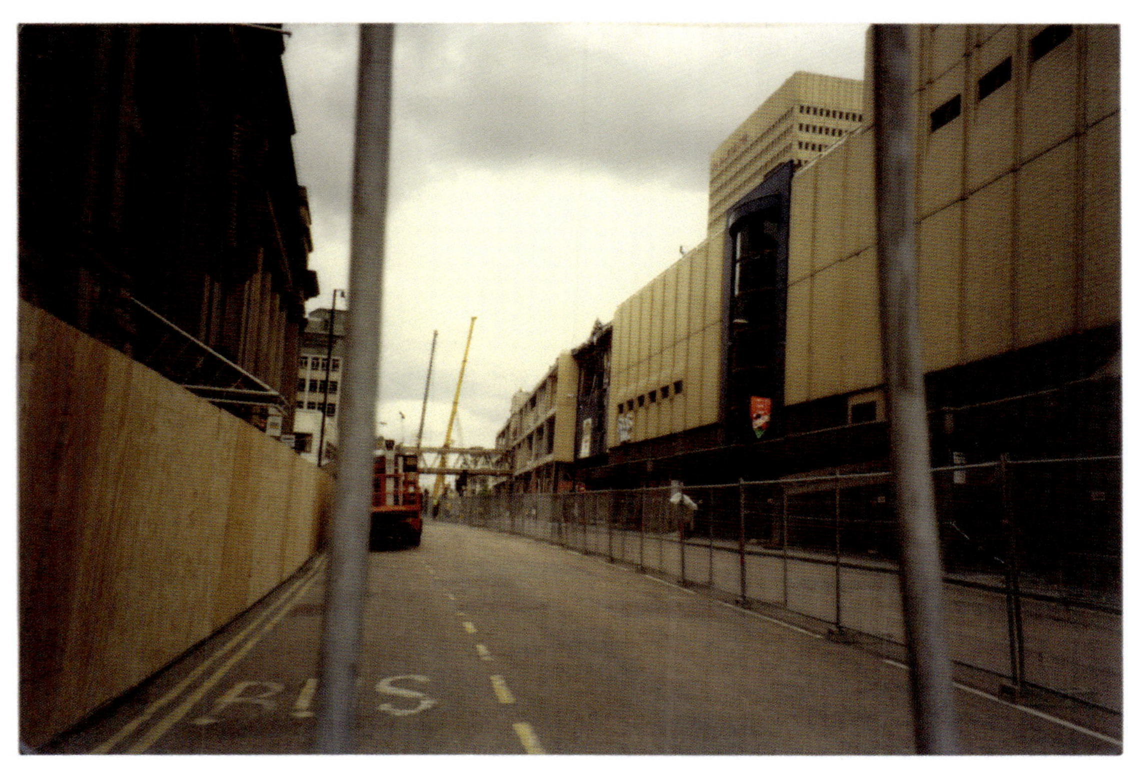

XXXVII

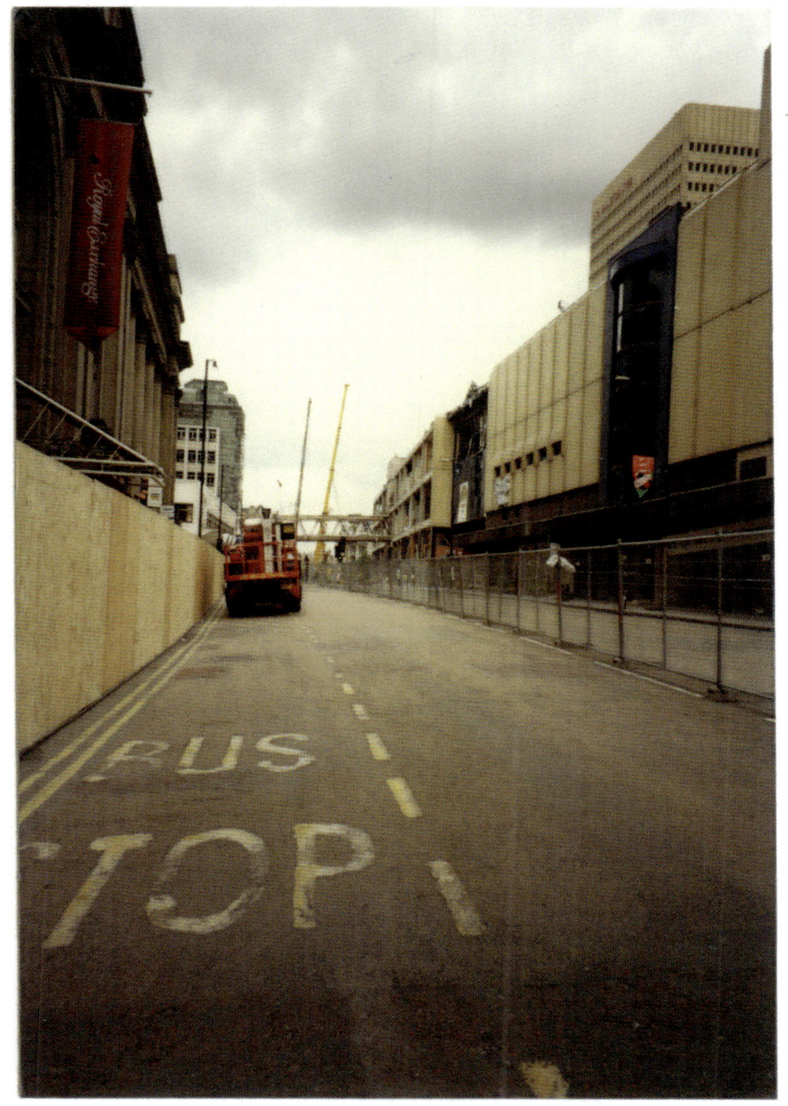
BUS
TOP

"A remarkable find, the book deals with the material in a dry and straightforward manner which I find reinforces the subtle drama of the pictures."
Jem Southam — author of *Four Winters, The Harbour* and *The Moth*

"An important and thought-provoking book. It is very well conceived. I appreciate the simple, honest way of presenting these found images and the succinct text. I like the natural beige cast that gives it such visual coherence. The mysterious provenance of the images adds to the eeriness."
Alison McCauley — author of *Shimmers* and *Anywhere but Here*

"This astonishing caché of photographs capture not the violent explosions of the '96 bomb, but its silent, eerie aftermath. Their stillness is akin to that of the eye of a storm, between the chaos of deindustrialisation and the speculative maelstrom of our own times. With cryptic origin, they are destined to become a cult touchstone for all who seek to understand New Manchester."
Isaac Rose — author of *The Rentier City: Manchester and the Making of the Neoliberal Metropolis*

3300

Edited by Nirvana Heire

Published by PARIAH PRESS 2024

PARIAH PRESS
pariahpress.com
pariahpress@gmail.com

British Library Cataloguing in Publication Data
Heire, Nirvana
3300

isbn 978-1-9196296-4-3 paperback

Set in MT Futura Now
Typesetting by PARIAH PRESS

Design by PARIAH PRESS and Nirvana Heire

Printed in Italy

Thank you: Ely Grey and Arthur Simpson